To:

From:

Bitch? Moi?

By Nancy Rider Hunt

Introduction by Barbara Paulding

 PETER PAUPER PRESS, INC.
White Plains, New York

*To my family, who provided me with great
material for this book, and especially to my mother,
who loved olive sandwiches and a good laugh!
She, however, was too classy and demure
to have said these kinds of things.*

Designed by Heather Zschock

Illustrations copyright © 2007 Olive Sandwiches, Inc.

Copyright © 2007
Peter Pauper Press, Inc.
202 Mamaroneck Avenue
White Plains, NY 10601
All rights reserved
ISBN 978-1-59359-864-8

Printed in China

7   6   5   4   3   2   1

Visit us at www.peterpauper.com

Bitch? Moi?

BITCH?

MOI?

Here is a retro tribute
to your inner bitch—

you know, the one
who's queen of all she
sees, the one who
takes no prisoners
when it comes to men,
the one who has a
wicked sense of humor
and knows how to use
it. Let these pages

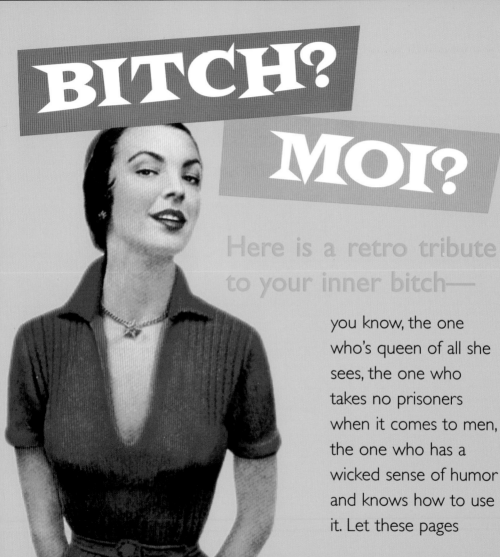

inspire you to add audacity to your attitude as you join the sisterhood that stands united under the motto, "It really *is* all about me!"

Join this madcap tour through the Land of Worthy Women, where the question "How much fun can I have before I go to hell?" is put to the test, and where men are welcome as long as they come fast, fun, and fully funded. Like a woman, this little book makes up with wit and grit what it may lack in size, with a knowing nod to the fact that being fabulous can be *so* exhausting.

Lest we be accused of harboring a sense of entitlement, let us assure you, dear reader, that our needs are really quite simple— "all we want is . . . everything!"

Gardening, yoga, bubble baths, medication... and I still want to smack somebody!

The queen is
not granting an
audience today.

The more I see of men,
the more I like my
pet squirrel.

Have I told you lately that you bug me?

I never met a man
I couldn't blame.

Remember, darling, jewelry prevents headaches.

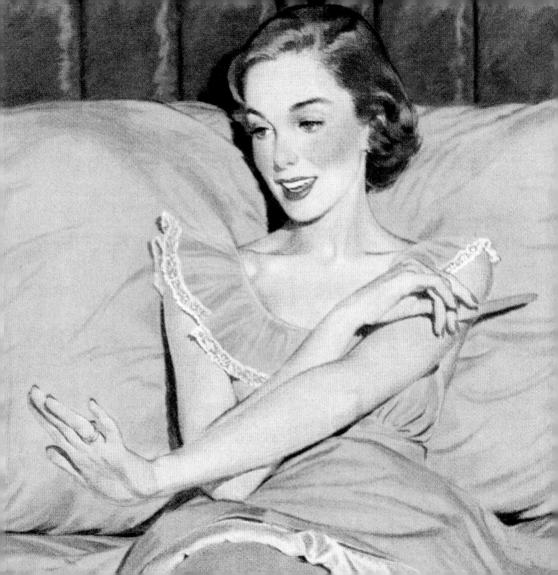

Back in my day, we hiked ten miles through the snow for sex & cigarettes!

She liked her men
fast, fun, and
fully funded!

When it came to
fish and men,
her motto was,
"catch and release."

He was a " Legend "
in his own mind
and a " Loser " in hers!

It was SO cold,
I almost got
married!

she didn't need a man...
she had all the peckers
she could handle!

Some say men
are just as sensitive as
women...

but who really cares?

We have nothing
against men,
but we're looking
for a cure!

I LIVE IN THE FAST LANE BUT I'M MARRIED TO A SPEED BUMP!

The problem with
"stud muffins"
is they don't
always rise!

She wasn't crazy about either one, but she liked a little competition.

*Just so you know,
I renewed my
backseat driver's
license!*

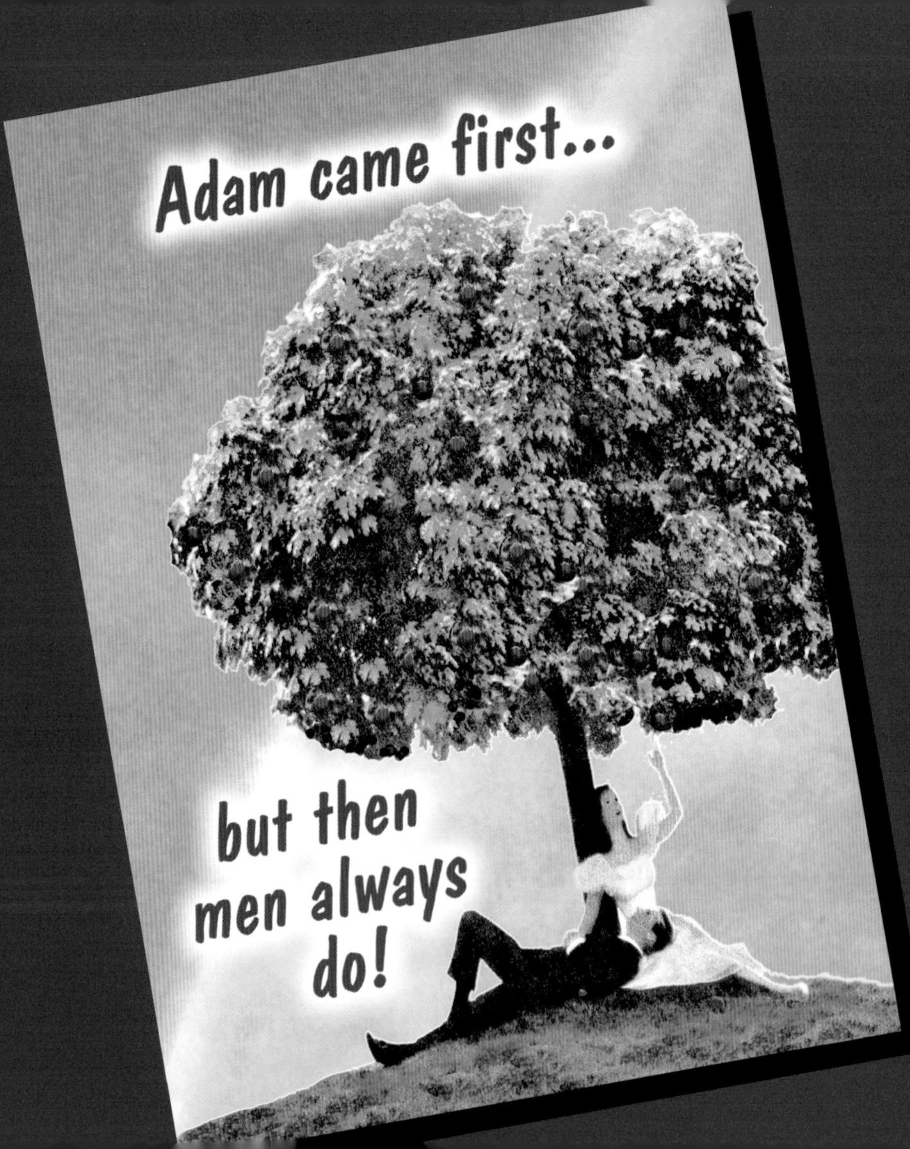
Adam came first...
but then
men always
do!

How can I miss
him if he won't
go away?

Never put off 'til tomorrow what your husband can do for you today!

Naughty boy!
Go to my room!

I daydream about someone to "do me" AND the laundry!